★"A sparkling homage to a diverse category of insect."
—*Publishers Weekly*, starred review

From the acclaimed duo **Dianna Hutts Aston** and
**Sylvia Long** comes this gorgeous look at the fascinating
world of beetles. From fireflies to rainbow scarab beetles,
an incredible variety of beetles are showcased here
in all their splendor. Poetic in voice and elegant in design,
this carefully researched book will spark the imaginations
of children in a classroom reading circle as well as on
a parent's lap.

## Also Available:

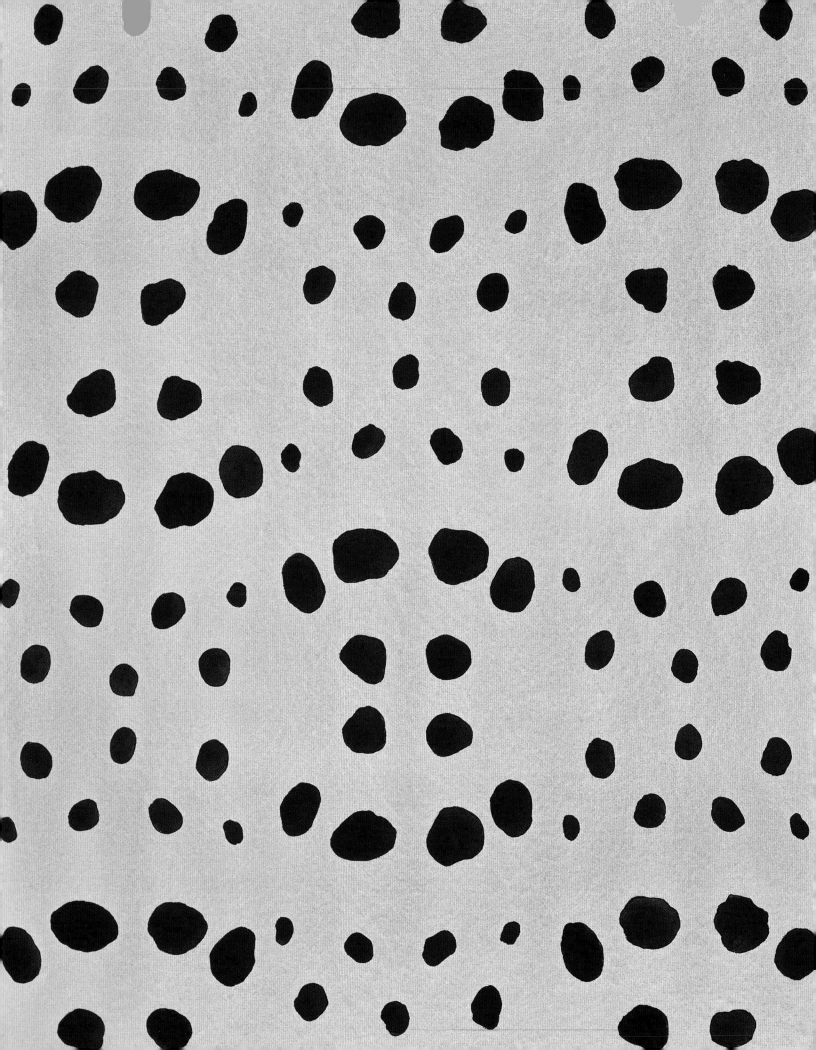

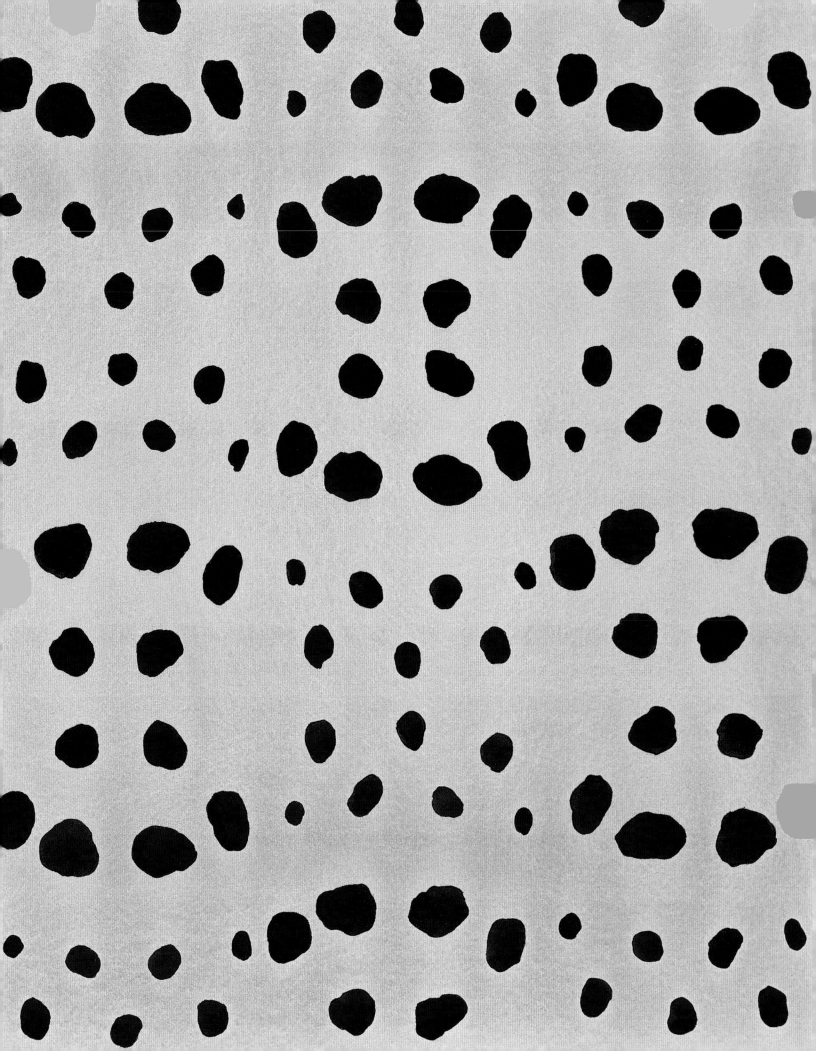

To the Ladybug Warriors —D. H. A.

To my son, John—more courageous, loving, kind,
and loyal than any mother could wish her son to be —S. L.

Special thanks to Lynn LeBeck.

First Chronicle Books LLC paperback edition, published in 2023.
Originally published in hardcover in 2016 by Chronicle Books LLC.

ISBN 978-1-7972-1587-7

The Library of Congress has cataloged the original edition under ISBN 978-1-4521-2712-5.

Manufactured in India.

FSC
www.fsc.org

MIX
Paper | Supporting
responsible forestry
FSC™ C016779

Original book design by Sara Gillingham Studio.
Paperback design by Sandy Frank.
Hand lettering by Anne Robin and Sylvia Long.
The illustrations in this book were rendered in watercolor.

10 9 8 7 6 5 4 3 2 1

Chronicle Books LLC
680 Second Street
San Francisco, California 94107

Chronicle Books—we see things differently.
Become part of our community at www.chroniclekids.com.

Rosalia Longicorn

Feather-horned Beetle

# A Beetle Is Shy

Dianna Hutts Aston + Sylvia Long

chronicle books · san francisco

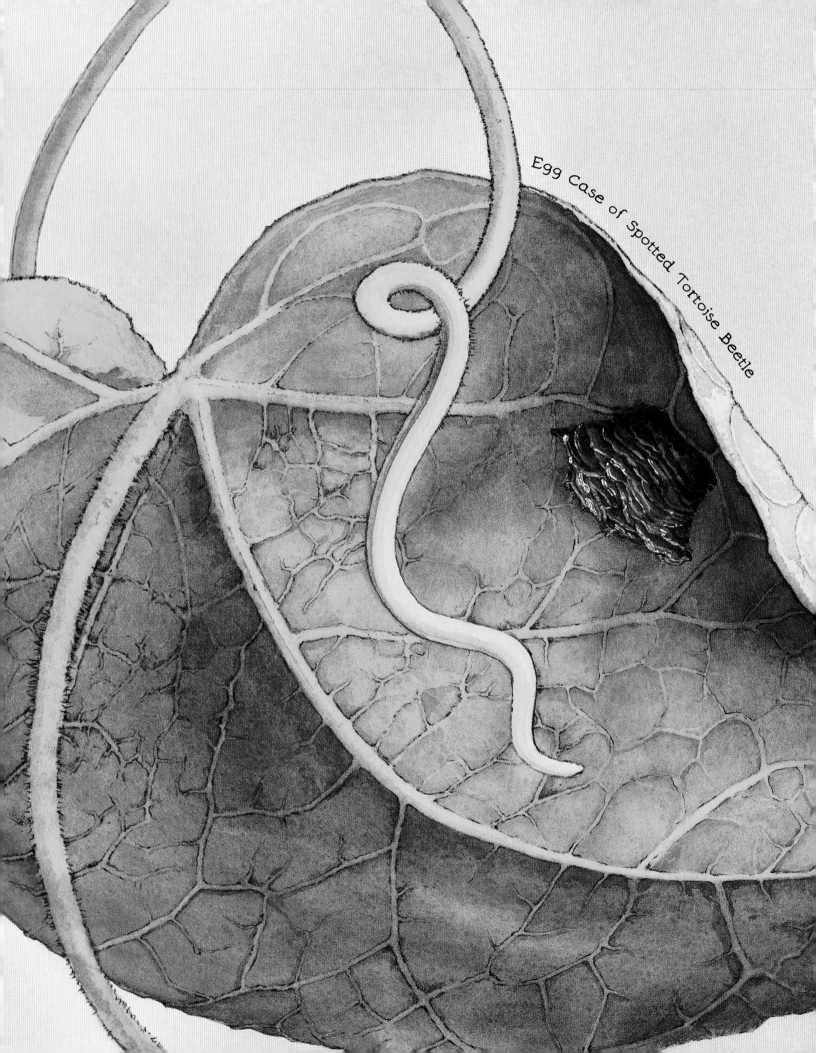

Egg Case of Spotted Tortoise Beetle

# A beetle is shy.

It begins its life inside an egg . . .
soft and wingless, tender,
protected by the roots of trees
and the undersides of leaves.

The egg hatches into a wriggling larva
that feasts on plant and animal matter,
growing quickly, shedding its hard outer skin,
or *exoskeleton*, many times as it gets bigger.

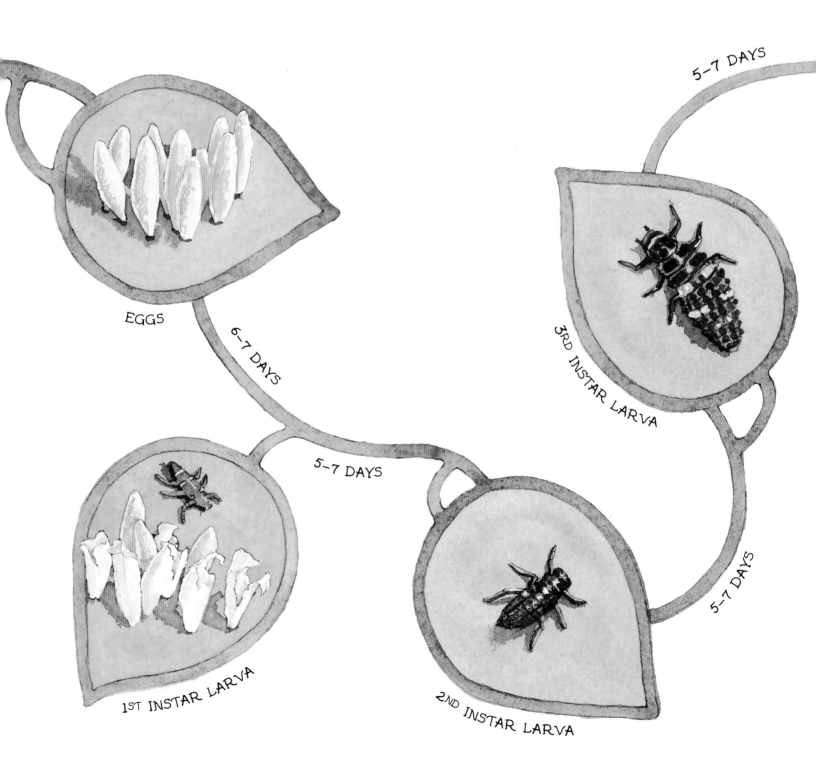

EGGS

6–7 DAYS

5–7 DAYS

1ST INSTAR LARVA

2ND INSTAR LARVA

3RD INSTAR LARVA

5–7 DAYS

5–7 DAYS

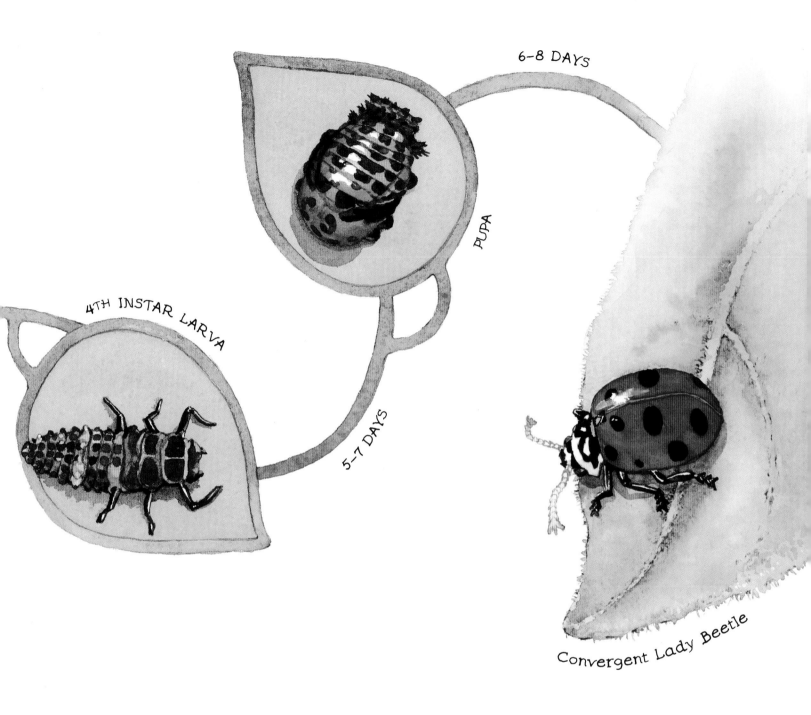

6-8 DAYS

PUPA

4TH INSTAR LARVA

5-7 DAYS

Convergent Lady Beetle

Then the larva begins its transformation in a cocoon-like
pupa, where it develops wings and antennae.
Finally, a beetle twists and turns, squirming free of the
pupa's leathery skin, and its body and true colors emerge.

Bumelia
Borer

Golden Target Beetle

Dead-nettle
Leaf Beetle

*A beetle is kaleidoscopic.*

Rainbow Stag Beetle

Goldstreifiger

Red-speckled Jewel Beetle

Emerald Ash Borer

While many beetles are black or brown, some are *iridescent*, or shimmery and rainbow-colored.

Cobalt Milkweed Beetle

# A beetle is colossal ...

Titan Beetle

One of the largest insects
in the world, the titan beetle,
has mandibles, or jaws,
powerful enough to snap
a pencil in half!

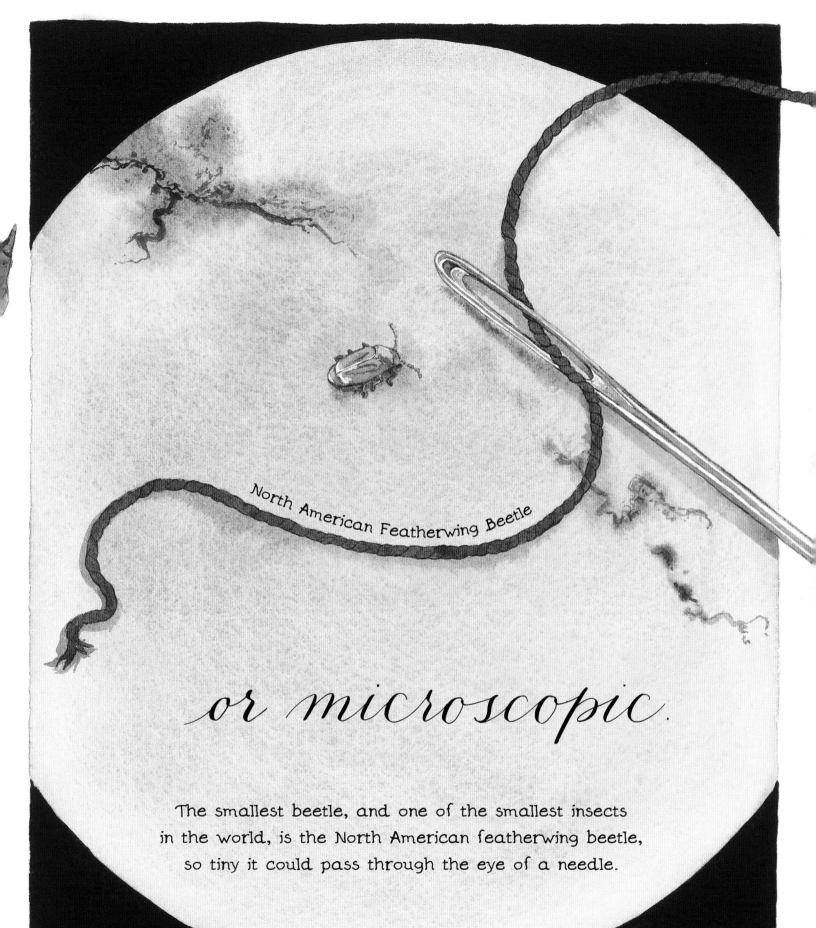

North American Featherwing Beetle

*or microscopic.*

The smallest beetle, and one of the smallest insects
in the world, is the North American featherwing beetle,
so tiny it could pass through the eye of a needle.

A beetle

INDIA
stag beetle chutney

VIETNAM
coconut tree beetle
larvae soup

THAILAND
wok-fried dung beetle

*is tasty.*

Beetles are found on every continent except Antarctica. Because they are so plentiful, and also protein-rich, they are eaten by humans all around the world.

In the United States, you can snack on mealworm ice cream. In the Netherlands, you can try chocolate infused with mealworms.

**PAPUA NEW GUINEA**
roasted palm weevil larvae

**AUSTRALIA**
roasted longhorn
beetle larvae

# A beetle is a digger...

Some have legs that are wide and jagged for digging. Dung beetles are like bulldozers, rolling marble-size balls of animal waste and burying them underground or on top of dung heaps.

Rainbow Scarab Beetle

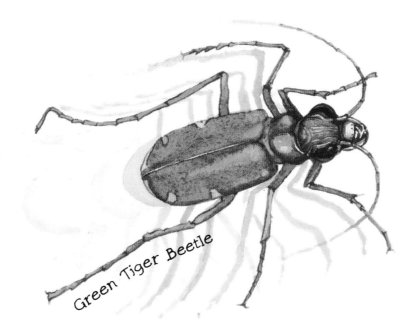

Green Tiger Beetle

## a runner . . .

Some beetles have long, slender legs made
for speed. The tiger beetle runs up to
2 feet (61 centimetres) per second. At that
rate, this Olympian of the insect world can run
50 yards (46 metres) in just over a minute.

Pigweed Flea Beetle

## a hopper . . .

Some beetles hop. Flea beetles use their toes to catapult
themselves about 13 inches (33 centimetres) high.

or a swimmer.

Aquatic beetles seek meals of algae, insects, worms, tadpoles, and even small fish. Some have flattened legs like paddles for swimming.

Others glide like sailboats atop
ponds and lakes, or speed
beneath the surface as if they
were skating on glass ceilings.

Water-gliding Rove Beetle

# A beetle is

Most beetles send messages to each other using chemicals called *pheromones*. The scent of pheromones acts as a code that tells beetles where to find mates or food. Others "talk" to each other with squeaky, raspy sounds made by scraping their wings against their bodies.

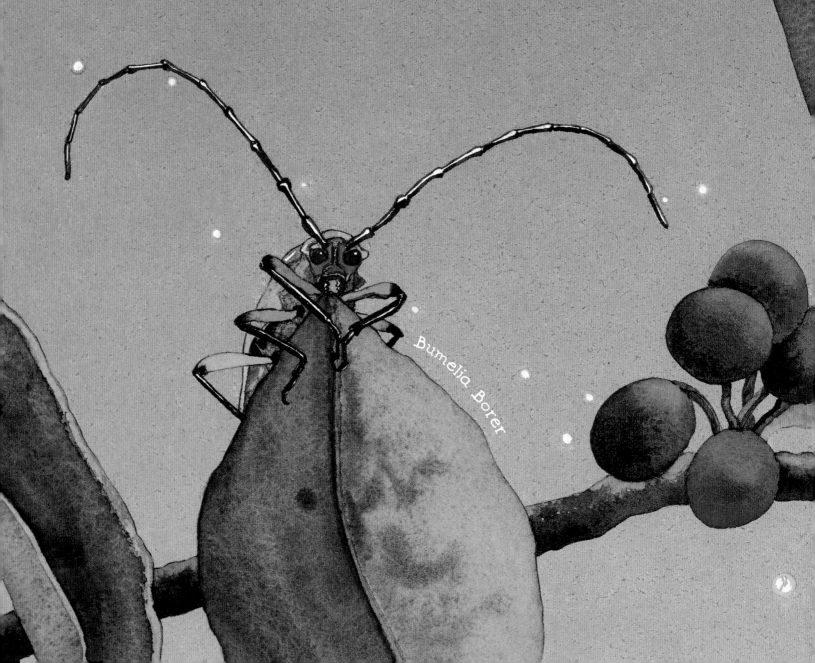

Bumelia Borer

# telegraphic.

Fireflies communicate by *bioluminescence*,
or glowing lights. They flash their signals
to attract a mate, defend their territory,
and warn away predators.

Firefly

Beetles keep themselves safe in many ways. The colors and shapes of some beetles, especially those that feed on plants, help them *camouflage* themselves, or hide among leaves and bark.

Acorn Weevil

*A beetle is guarded.*

Some beetles protect themselves by emitting a liquid that is *toxic*, or poisonous. True to its name, the blister beetle secretes a toxin that burns the skin and causes swelling.

Blister Beetle

Arrow-poison beetles are so poisonous that hunters in some African tribes use the juice these beetles secrete on the tips of their small arrows to kill large animals.

Arrow-poison Beetle

LARVA

Wasp Beetle

Beetles also protect themselves through *mimicry*—using color and shape to warn away enemies. For instance, one type of harmless longhorn beetle looks like a wasp.

Bombardier Beetle

One kind of beetle, the bombardier beetle, releases a boiling spray that changes into gas, which stings the eyes and creates a smokescreen to confuse its enemies.

Convergent Lady Beetle

# A beetle is helpful...

Lady beetles, also known
as ladybugs or ladybird beetles,
and soldier beetles help keep
plants healthy by eating aphids.

Soldier Beetle

Striped Cucumber Beetle

Boll Weevil

*or harmful.*

Weevils and other beetles eat the leaves, stems, and roots of plants, destroying many crops that humans rely on, such as corn, lettuce, wheat, cotton, and potatoes. In homes, spider beetles, about the size of a grain of rice, feed on wool, cereal, spices, bread, dried fruit—even pet food!

Spider Beetle

A beetle is prehistoric.

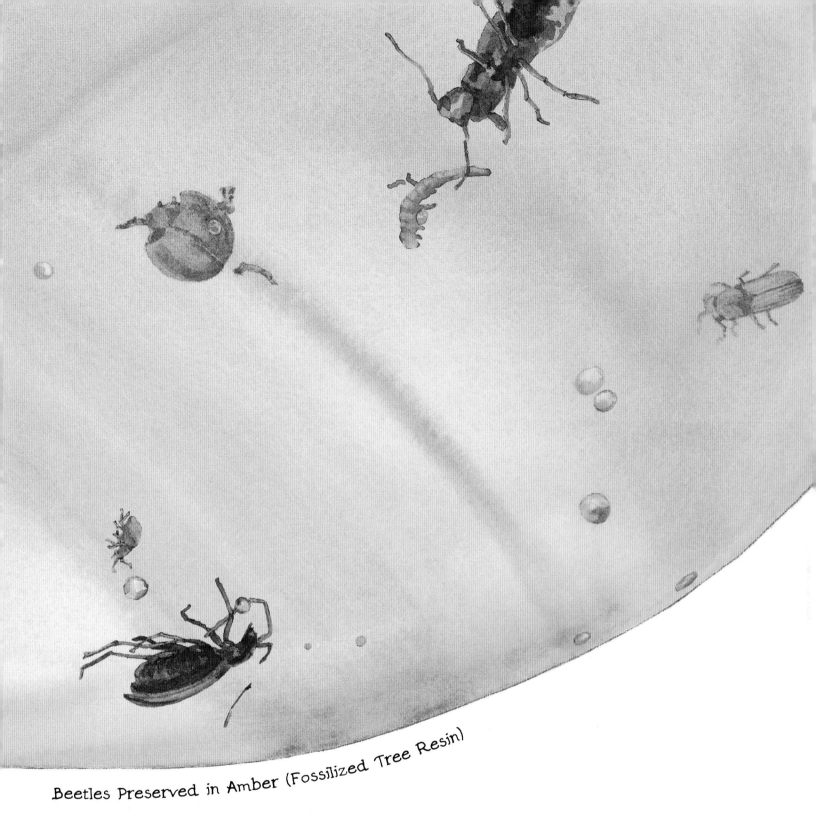

Beetles Preserved in Amber (Fossilized Tree Resin)

Fossils show that beetles inhabited Earth
when dinosaurs did, almost 300 million
years ago, making them millions of years
older than butterflies, bees, and other insects.

Red-speckled
Jewel Beetle

ABDOMEN

ELYTRON (HARD OUTER WING)

There are more than 1 million known species of insects on Earth, which is more than half of all known animal species. Nearly half of insects are beetles. Unlike other winged insects, beetles have a pair of hard outer wings called *elytra* that shield their delicate inner flight wings against heat, rain, and hungry predators.

A beetle is armored.

FLIGHT WING

Spotted Tortoise Beetle Pupa

*A beetle is shy...*

A newborn, soft and hungry,
hurries to seal itself into a cocoon,
where it can be still and cozy until
it becomes what it was meant to be.

*And then...*

a beetle
is bold!

Spotted Tortoise Beetle

Pigweed Flea Beetle

Bumelia Borer

Dead-nettle Leaf Beetle

North American Featherwing Beetle

Rainbow Stag Beetle

Feather-horned Beetle

Wasp Beetle

Firefly

Red-speckled Jewel Beetle

Bombardier Beetle

Arrow-poison Beetle

Boll Weevil

Goldstreifiger

Striped Cucumber Beetle

Convergent Lady Beetle

Green Tiger Beetle

Cobalt Milkweed Beetle

Titan Beetle

Spotted Tortoise Beetle

Water-gliding Rove Beetle

Blister Beetle

Emerald Ash Borer

Rainbow Scarab Beetle

Soldier Beetle

Acorn Weevl

Rosalia Longicorn

Spider Beetle

Golden Target Beetle

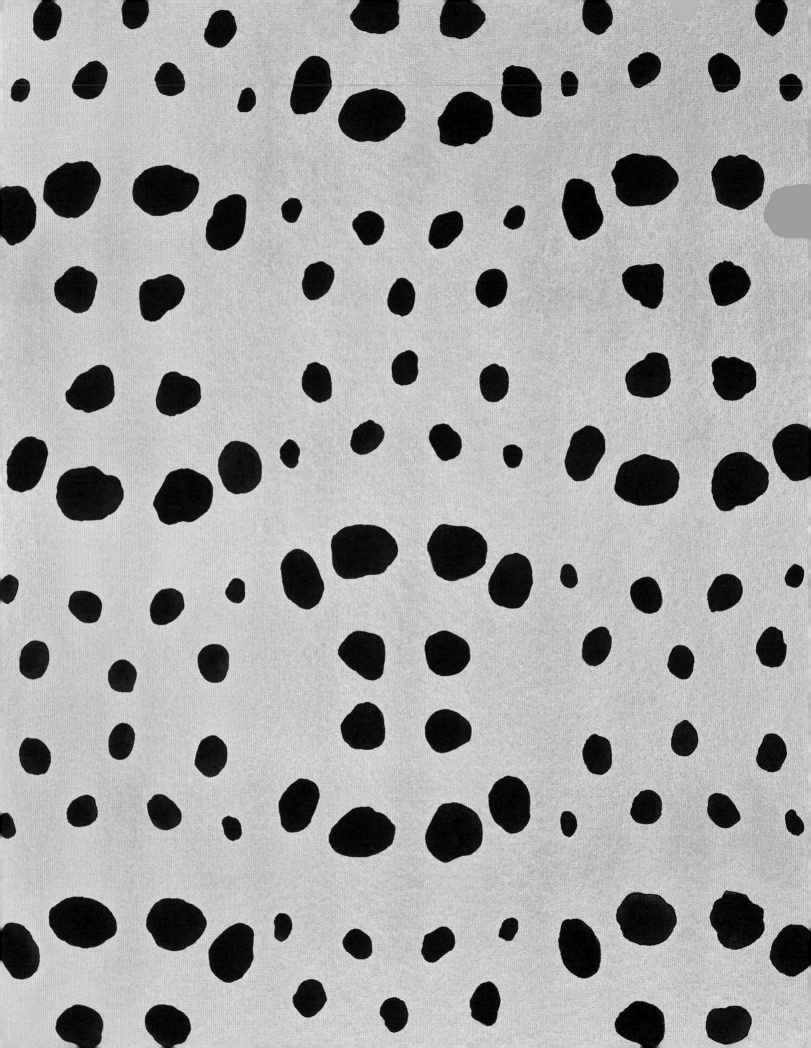

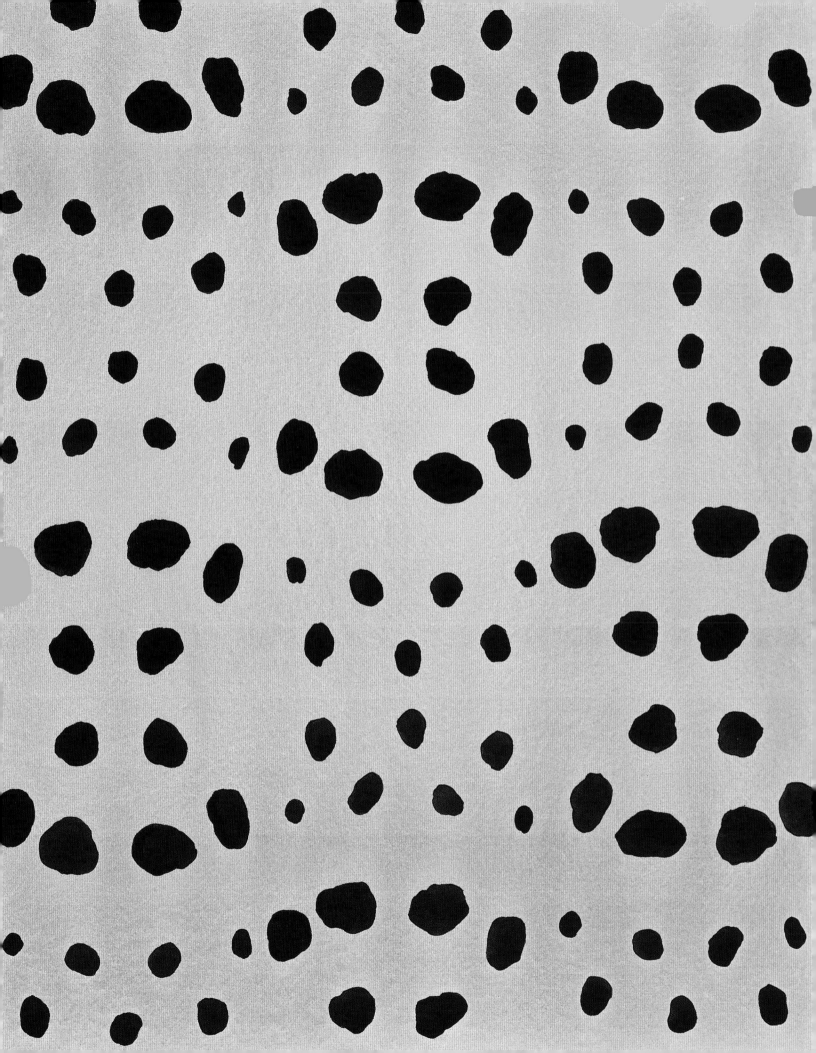

# ALSO BY DIANNA HUTTS ASTON AND SYLVIA LONG:

## An Egg Is Quiet

★"A delight for budding naturalists of all stripes, flecks, dots, and textures."
—*Kirkus Reviews*, starred review

"Will inspire kids to marvel." —*Booklist*

A Junior Library Guild Premiere selection
One of Scholastic *Parent & Child* magazine's 100 Greatest Books for Kids

## A Butterfly Is Patient

★"Both eye-catching and informative." —*School Library Journal*, starred review

★"A lovely mix of science and wonder." —*Publishers Weekly*, starred review

★"Stunning." —*Library Media Connection*, starred review

An ALA Notable Children's Book
An NSTA Outstanding Science Trade Book for Students K–12
An NCTE Notable Children's Book in the Language Arts

## A Rock Is Lively

"A visual and verbal feast." —*Boston Globe*

★"Eye-catching and eye-opening." —*School Library Journal*, starred review

An IRA Teachers' Choices Reading List selection

## A Seed Is Sleepy

★"Will stretch children's minds and imaginations." —*School Library Journal*, starred review

An IRA Teachers' Choices Reading List selection

## A Nest Is Noisy

"Beautiful . . . an asset to science collections." —*Booklist*

A Junior Library Guild selection

DIANNA HUTTS ASTON has written many bestselling children's books inspired by her awe for the wonders of nature. She lives in the Texas Hill Country, where she is a student of wildflower seed harvesting and viticulture, a caregiver, and a chauffeur.

SYLVIA LONG is the illustrator of many award-winning books for children that have sold more than 2.5 million copies. Her detailed paintings are inspired by her love of animals and the outdoors. She lives in Scottsdale, Arizona. Visit her at www.sylvia-long.com.